CLUTTER
REHAB

101

*Tips and Tricks to Become
an Organization Junkie
and Love It!*

Laura Wittmann

Ulysses Press

For Miranda, Sarah, Joy and Annie,
my sisters in Christ who believed I could do this
from the very beginning and provided the encouragement,
laughter, and prayer that I needed to pull it off.
Thanks for putting up with my crazy!

Published in the U.S. by
ULYSSES PRESS
P.O. Box 3440
Berkeley, CA 94703
www.ulyssespress.com

ISBN: 978-1-56975-863-2
Library of Congress Control Number 2010937117

Printed in the United States by Bang Printing

2 4 6 8 10 9 7 5 3 1

Acquisitions Editor: Keith Riegert
Managing Editor: Claire Chun
Project Manager: Kelly Reed
Editor: Anna Dizon
Proofreader: Lauren Harrison
Production: Alice Riegert, Abigail Reser
Design and layout: what!design @ whatweb.com
Cover photos: shutterstock.com / © Camilla Wisbauer, ©qingqing
Interior photos: see page 127

Distributed by Publishers Group West

Contents

Clutter rehab 7

Let's talk clutter 9

1 Ask clutter questions 15

2 Banish clutter excuses 16

3 Consolidate...everything! 19

4 Remember: less is more 20

5 Give everything a designated space............................ 21

6 Create simple solutions for keys.............................. 23

7 Don't make a system too complicated 24

8 Have a daily walkabout 25

9 Never leave a room empty-handed 26

10 Take pictures of sentimental clutter 27

11 Place wire shelves in cupboards............................... 29

12 Put vertical dividers in kitchen cupboards.................... 29

13 Use containers to set limits and boundaries 30

14 Select containers to create more space 31

15 Organizing doesn't have to be expensive—make do 32

16 Create a backpack station 33

17 Set up a beverage station...................................... 34

18 Have a donation station.. 35

19 Designate a craft center station............................... 36

20 Create a game station... 37

21 Design a gift-wrapping station 38

22 Utilize an "I'm outta here" shelf 39

23 Use hooks for kid's coats instead of hangers 40

24 Attach hooks on the back of doors for extra storage 40

25 Get kids involved with organizing............................. 42

26 Start every week with a menu plan 43

27 Set a grocery shopping day and stick to it..................... 44

28 Have a central calendar your whole family can access....... 45

29 Create a visual calendar for young kids 46

30 If you don't like something, change it
or stop complaining 47

31 Establish a "command center"................................. 48

32 Re-purpose items for creative storage solutions............. 49

33 Use labels to know what goes where 50

34 Color code the kids.. 51

35 Do a "ten-minute tidy" every night before bed.............. 52

36 Mark expiration dates on makeup............................. 53

37 Keep flat surfaces clear... 54

38 Work together with a friend for inspiration
and motivation 55

39 Don't keep out-of-season clothes in prime
real estate space.. 56

40 Purge clothing at the end of the season,
not the beginning... 57

41 Learn these eleven tips for parting with your clothes....... 59

42 Use the "one in, one out" rule 61

43 Keep toy sets together in specific rooms..................... 62

44 Use toy boxes only for large items............................ 63

45 Schedule regular toy "clean-outs" 64

56 Toss your junk mail right away................................. 65

47 Utilize notebooks and lists 66

48 Set your daily top three to-dos 67

49 Don't look up.. 68

50 If you haven't used something in a year, get rid of it 69

51 If it doesn't fit the vision for the space, get rid of it 70

52 Keep a wastebasket in every room 71

53 Cut the knick-knacks out....................................... 72

54 Set your own clutter standards.................................. 73

55 Store stuff where you use it...................................... 74

56 Use memory binders or totes to organize
kids' keepsakes 75

57 Do not keep more than three months' backlog
of magazine articles... 76

58 Keep manuals with the receipt stapled to them
all in one place 77

59 Pack activity bags 78

60 Keep your vehicle stocked with essentials..................... 80

61 Use a purse organizer or clear bags to organize
your purse or bag 81

62 Embrace Plan B and let go of perfectionism................. 82

63 Keep projects in progress under control 83

64 Disguise your storage.. 84

65 Use rolling plastic drawer units 85

66 Implement a weekly cleaning schedule 86

67 Create a "Housekeeping Mission Statement" 88

68 Have a handy library basket 89

69 Limit your family to two towels and two sets
of sheets per person 90

70 Use space bags 91

71 Utilize online photo books for pictures...................... 92

72 Create a "to file" basket.. 93

73 Use pizza boxes for scrapbook paper or
children's artwork... 94

74 Use visual cues to eliminate clutter. 95

75 Install closet organizers 97

76 Create a binder and online folder for recipes 98

77 Use drawer dividers... 99

78 Designate a charging station 100

79 Make a jewelry organizer...................................... 101

80 Think about your habits 102

81 Label the lids of spices 103

82 Make a rule: no food in bedrooms 104

83 Use a system to organize kid clothes 106

84 Tackle small tasks to get big results 107

85 Regularly go through the medicine cabinet
for expired products 108

86 Stop sorting your laundry.................................... 109

87 Organize coupons... 110

88 Streamline kitchen utensils 111

89 Organize your pantry 112

90 Create an e-mail folder system 113

91 Cut the clutter in your bedroom and create
the sanctuary you deserve 114

92 Invite company over as motivation 115

93 Use binder clips for cables.................................. 115

94 Use Command Hooks to save space 116

95 Keep toothbrushes organized 117

96 Use camera bags for video games 118

97 Don't put it off until later 119

98 Organize your entryway 121

99 Focus!... 122

100 Organize while watching TV.............................. 123

101 Use multitasking wisely 125

Epilogue.. 126

Photo credits 127

About the author 128

Clutter Rehab

LET ME START RIGHT OFF by admitting my little secret: I'm an organization addict. Yes, it's true! But this doesn't mean I have all my soup cans lined up in pretty little rows with their labels facing out, my spices alphabetized, or perfectly color-coordinated bins and baskets. My sheets aren't folded and stacked pristinely, and I don't make my kids sort their Legos by color!

What's important to me is being organized just enough (notice I didn't say perfectly) so that I can enjoy the rewards of organization without complicating life more than I need to. I avoid stress and chaos as much as possible with strategies that help me eliminate clutter, prepare for life's little mishaps, save money, and maximize my time so that I can run my household efficiently. This is the freedom that comes from a simplified, organized way of life. Sound impossible?

It isn't! Over the past five years, I have taken a journey toward simplicity and organization and learned some valuable and practical lessons along the way. What started me on my journey? A new baby, a job loss, and a transition to becoming a work-from-home mom, all at the same time. It was overwhelming, to say the least, but it was also what opened my eyes to how out of control my life had become. I just didn't stop to think about how stressed I was. It wasn't until I slowly started the transition to a simpler lifestyle and began introducing some of the changes outlined in this book that I realized how chaotic my life had actually been before. My husband and I made adjustments to how we did things: got the kids involved around the house, scheduled fewer activities, developed simple organizing processes and systems, and, most of all, we reduced our clutter. Believe me, it certainly didn't all happen overnight. Rather, it was a gradual process that continues to this day.

I document my ongoing journey on my blog, *I'm an Organizing Junkie* (www.orgjunkie.com), which I started in 2006 as a way to share this passion of mine with others. As my blog has grown, I've realized I'm not alone in my desire to live an organized life, and nothing makes me happier than the thrill of watching others experience this high of organizing and the life-changing benefits that go along with it. Yet what we all have to remember is that organizing isn't a means to an end, *it's an ongoing process.* Just when you think you've got things all figured out at the top of the ride, the roller coaster of life dips down and spins you in another direction. However, with consistent practice and a good seat belt, you'll learn to expect those dips and turns and be ready for them. You'll have strategies and systems in place, not necessarily to prevent life's curveballs, but to keep you securely fastened so you can go with the flow and maintain your sanity along the way. Organizing is a fun addiction with amazing results and, hopefully, after reading this book, you'll be well on your way to becoming an organizing junkie as well. ENJOY THE RIDE!

Let's Talk Clutter

Throughout this book we're going to be talking about clutter.

Clutter = Anything you don't love or use or have the space to store

What is it about our stuff that seems to cause it to multiply in the night? Too much stuff and too little space results in clutter. You can either get rid of some stuff or find more space. In my opinion, getting rid of stuff is a lot less expensive and a lot less work than finding more space, especially if that space comes in the form of a storage unit or a bigger house. These are choices we all have to make and, truthfully, clutter is so much more than just the storage solutions needed to contain it. Dealing with clutter requires making some tough decisions on a regular basis.

Clutter = Procrastinated decisions

It's not easy making these decisions because we get attached to our stuff. We fear the consequences of getting rid of something and we wonder if we'll regret it later, if we'll lose the memory associated with it, or if we'll hurt someone's feelings. But the truth is this: Clutter is immobilizing. It stifles our freedom to enjoy the spaces we do have, it takes up mental space whether we know it or not, and it can be a huge source of stress and frustration, which then plays itself out in so many other areas of our lives. Making decisions with potential consequences is always hard, but choosing to make no decision at all or putting it off until later when you think the decision-making process is going to be easier isn't going to help you. Stuff doesn't go away on its own; it just continues to pile up.

Luckily, the skills required to deal with our clutter and organize it all are skills anyone can learn. Yes, some of us may be more adept at it, but like anything else, with regular practice, the process gets faster and easier each time. Remember to keep in mind that the goal here is not perfection. The goal is simply to make life easier and more efficient, and to reduce stress (not add to it) by using easily maintained systems that allow for an uncluttered space, an uncluttered mind, and an uncluttered life.

The benefits of letting go of clutter far outweigh the anxiety you feel in the moment.

Believe it can be done! Consider this your clutter rehab, and I'm going to teach you how!

Where to start?

I think so many of us look around our spaces and get simply overwhelmed. You know you want to make a change, but aren't sure where to start or how to move forward. That feeling can be paralyzing and often leads to procrastination. The straightforward answer to this question is to *start small*. If you have a whole room needing attention, break the job down into manageable bits. Perhaps you start with just one drawer or the closet. Start with what frustrates you the most. Follow my organizing process below and the tips in this book and you'll be well on your way to organizing success. With each accomplishment, revel in what you've achieved! It's a big deal, so be proud and use that as motivation to continue on.

The Organizing PROCESS

Organizing is an ongoing *process* and not a destination. Just when you think you've got a handle on things, it's time to do it all over again. Life happens. Kids outgrow their toys and clothes, your responsibilities and needs change, you have another child, get married, start a new job, and on and on. With the right techniques, however, you can stay on top of these things. You can control your space rather than have your space control you. Being organized allows you to quickly restore the situation when the ride gets a little bumpy.

PROCESS is an easy acronym I've created to allow you to break down any organizing project into simple, straightforward steps. Using it will help you stick to a plan and achieve optimal organizing results. In fact, by following the PROCESS steps below, anyone can conquer any space of any size. Do one step at a time or all at once, depending on the time you have available for the task.

Here are the PROCESS steps:

Plan of attack: Plan your project before you start. First, evaluate your present system. You need to know what isn't working for you to help you determine how you'd like the space to function. Next, set a budget and make a time line. Get clear about how much money and time you're willing to invest before you get started. Definitely don't just jump in blind; you'll set yourself up for failure if you do.

Remove items: Empty the space completely so you can start from a clean slate. I know this sounds like more work, but it's so much more effective than just shuffling everything around. Removing items from where they've been stored will give you a fresh perspective on the space you want organized. It will enable you to re-evaluate how you want the space to look. You can't do this when the area is cluttered up with stuff.

Organize into piles: One each to donate/toss/sell/keep/relocate. Sort like with like; this will result in many piles around you, but don't stop to deal with them until your sort is complete. Then tackle each pile one by one. Purge excess: The more you purge, the less you have to find a home for. Your goal is to bring back into your space only what you love and use and can fit into the space you have available.

Containerize: Containers and other storage solutions establish limits and boundaries; they designate a space for items being kept. Consolidate where possible.

Evaluate your plan: How is your system working for you? Are you able to work your system? What needs to be modified? A good system should be easy to maintain.

Solve and Simplify any remaining issues: Address anything that isn't working for you and revise accordingly.

The 101 organizing tips you'll find in this book, along with the PROCESS steps I just outlined, are designed to take you on a journey toward clutter-free, simplified living. The tips are in no particular order, so feel free to work your way through them as is or to jump around as you see fit. I've intermingled simple clutter-control techniques that you'll be able to implement right away, along with some more involved tactics that might require additional time and a few adjustments in order to make them work for *your* family. Take it one tip at a time, and before you know it, you'll be on the other side of the chaos mountain.

SMILE, RELAX, AND ENJOY YOUR HARD WORK!

1

Ask clutter questions

As you face each clutter decision, ask yourself the questions below. You can do this in two ways. One is to evaluate each item by asking all the questions about it at once. If the thought of that seems too overwhelming, you can ask them in stages. For example, evaluate each item by going through and only asking the first question. Then take that same pile and go through the items again asking the second question, and so on. By the time you answer all five questions, your pile should be considerably smaller (if you've been honest, that is!).

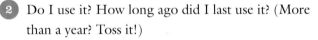

1. Do I love it?

2. Do I use it? How long ago did I last use it? (More than a year? Toss it!)

3. Do I have the room to store it without it affecting my efficiency and stress levels?

4. Am I willing to give up something else in order to make room for it?

5. Can I imagine myself or anyone else in my family ever loving it or using it in the foreseeable future?

2

Banish clutter excuses

Once you have your plan in place and your stuff removed, grab yourself three big bins or boxes to help you with the organize/sort part of PROCESS. Alternatively, you could use different colored garbage bags. Label one for *keep*, one for *donate/sell*, and one for *relocate* to another area of the house. You'll also need a garbage bag for trash. As you're doing your

sort, quickly make decisions about where each item you handle should go. If the decision is a really tough one, you may choose to pass and continue on. Limit yourself to three passes for the duration of your project. Those decisions will get easier for you as you start to feel the "high" of purging. Address each item and the excuses that pop into your head about why an item should stay. Is your excuse reasonable? Only you can be the judge of that.

Here's how you can combat some of those excuses in order to fight your desire to hold on to something:

I might need it one day.

That may be true, but if you haven't used it in a year, chances are you won't need it anytime soon. You have to weigh the cost between the prime real estate space it takes up and the cost to replace it if you do need to purchase it again in the future.

I don't want to hurt anyone's feelings by getting rid of it.

Fair enough, but I would assume the person you don't want to hurt is close to you or otherwise you wouldn't be so concerned about their feelings. If that's the case, then how much worse do you think this person would feel knowing the additional stress they've put you under? If you're keeping something to avoid hurting someone's feelings, you're essentially being a storage house for them. You are giving up storage space in *your* own home to make *them* happy. I'm sure you can think of many different ways to effectively use your space. Do not be burdened by stuff you're keeping for someone else.

I don't want to seem ungrateful.

It's all about heart: If your heart is in the right place, the giver will hopefully understand. You need to do what's right for you and your family. You don't always have to tell the giver that you and the item are parting ways. Re-gifting is a popular choice for new items, as is donating items to thrift stores. Take it to the thrift store in the next town if you're really worried about it! And don't forget places like Craigslist, eBay, or Freecycle. Whatever you do, don't hang on to something out of a sense of obligation—it just creates resentment.

It was so expensive.
Ah yes, the big-ticket item we just had to have—and there it sits collecting dust. It happens to all of us. You know you'll never get back what you paid for it, but remember, that item is taking up space in your house that could be better used for something else, which makes THAT piece of real estate more expensive than the item you are hanging on to!

The item could be valuable.
It's not worth anything if it's just sitting in a box that you don't have the room to store. If it isn't something you love or use regularly, get rid of it and make some money on it now.

It brings back so many memories.
Oh, emotional attachment. This one is probably the biggest culprit that holds people back. Our memories are often so wrapped up in physical material possessions that it becomes unbearable to part with something. I can understand that and I'm not opposed to keeping those things as long as you have the space available to store them. If you don't, try taking a picture of the item and allow the picture to conjure up the memory for you instead (see Tip 10).

3

Consolidate...everything!

I absolutely adore containers of all shapes and sizes because of how useful they are for consolidating. Anytime I can consolidate many things into one thing, thereby

taking up less space, it makes me a very happy girl. This tip works particularly well in the kitchen, where we can often find multiples of the same product open at the same time. Whenever I see this happening in my cupboard, I know my family is trying to mess with me because they know it drives me crazy. Empty smaller sizes of similar packages out into one bigger container. For instance, keep a snack basket handy in your pantry to house granola bars, fruit leathers, etc. You'll notice that once you eliminate bulky packaging, you end up with a lot more space in your cupboard. In addition, if we don't store "like with like," we forget what we have and

purchase more, which adds up to more money spent at the store. CONSOLIDATING IS ADDICTIVE!

4

Remember: less is more

This is the mind-set that took me the longest to obtain on my simplification journey, and I've finally got it. Less stuff means less to organize. Less clutter means less to clean. Fewer activities mean less running around and more family time. Less stuff means less money spent. Less clutter means less time

wasted. The bottom line is that less mess equals less stress! If you're having trouble letting go of the clutter, think about what you have to give up in order to hang on to these things. What is truly important to you? MAKE IT HAPPEN.

5

Give everything a designated space

How much time do you waste in a day looking for something? Seriously, you should add it up sometime. If you can't find something that you need in less than two or three minutes, you're wasting time. Think about it: If every day you spend ten minutes looking for your keys or your glasses or your wallet, over a one-year period you're wasting 60 hours of your time! That's more hours than a standard work week. Yikes! The reason we're losing these things in the first place is that we don't put them in the same spot each time. You come home from a long day at work, walk in the door, throw your keys on the table, and start opening the mail. The kids come home from school and throw their papers on the table as well. Soon those poor keys are buried under piles of paper. Then, as you're preparing dinner, your daughter goes to set the table and sweeps everything off the table and onto the counter. After dinner, you go to clean up the dinner mess, take one look at the paper pile, shake your head in frustration, and throw the whole pile into your office. Unfortunately, en route to the office, your keys fall out into a laundry basket full of clothes waiting to be washed and you don't even notice. Later in the evening, you head out to a meeting and—surprise—can't find your keys. You spend ten minutes tearing the house apart, yelling at the kids, becoming increasingly stressed as you realize that now you're late for your meeting. Do you see how easily this stress and frustration could have been avoided just by having a designated spot to put something down? Pick a place and use it consistently. Eventually, it will become a routine. YOU'LL BE GLAD YOU DID!

6

Create simple solutions for keys

Use a carabiner clip! I never lose my keys anymore since I began using this little trick. I keep one on each of my key rings, making it easy to attach my keys, when not in use, to my purse or wallet. This way, before I even get out of the van, I clip my keys onto my purse. I never have to wonder what I did with them. They're always there. So easy! When I venture out without my purse or bag, I can just clip my keys to my belt loop. What did this peace of mind cost me? A mere $1 from the Dollar Store! Who knew something so simple could provide so much sanity and order, not to mention freedom. Other solutions: Put a key hook next to the door or a basket on an entry table.

7

Don't make a system too complicated

If where you need to put something requires too much time and effort, you're defeating the purpose. Often, piles are piles because things don't have a designated space. Other times, it's because they do have a home and yet it takes too much time to put them there, so you pile things up to deal with later. I see stress in either scenario, as both result in piles. Piles result in misplaced items, misplaced items result in wasted time, wasted time results in frustration, frustration results in being overwhelmed, and being overwhelmed results in nothing getting done because we're too overwhelmed with the piles. Whew, what a cycle! Stop the madness and *simplify*. If the space designated for your kid's artwork requires you to sort it by day, then month, then year, by category, you may find you never get around to doing it. The artwork piles up until you can find the time to sort it all out. Only the time is never found so the pile grows and grows and grows. Your designated space and system (while great in theory) is much too complicated. Re-think your system so it works for you. Perhaps having just one box per year or even one box total and just writing the date on the back of each piece would work better for you.

8

Have a daily walkabout

In our house, we have a saying that triggers an instant flurry of activity. As is normal for most homes, items seem to magically wander from their normal "place of residence" to another area of the house. So when this momma hollers out, "Time for a walkabout!" the kids know it's time to for them to walk around the house picking up any of their stray items

that are out of place. It could be a stray sock, books, toys, hair elastics, paper, anything. It's not a huge overhaul, but *it simply means that items are collected from one room and put back into their proper home in another room.* Because we have a designated space for everything, the process is quick and painless and takes only a couple of minutes, but the results are huge. If you have smaller children, setting a timer works well for this. It saves me from having to constantly pick up after the kids and from always nagging at them, too!

9

Never leave a room empty-handed

It isn't earth-shattering, but it is the one thing that helps me stay on top of clutter and reign in the chaos from out-of-place "stuff." I never go from one floor to the next or one room to the next empty-handed. It's become a habit for me to check the space I'm leaving in anticipation of what can be put away in the space that I'm going to. It saves me time in the long run because I'm not leaving it all to pile up somewhere to deal with later, but instead making it a regular part of my day.

10

Take pictures of sentimental clutter

I mentioned before that the biggest reason we hang onto stuff is the memories attached to the item. Looking at it is what keeps the memory alive for us, and many are fearful that getting rid of an item means we'll be getting rid of the memory. The memory is inside of us, not in the object itself, although I do agree that it helps to have a memory trigger. The next time you're going through some of your sentimental clutter, ask yourself if perhaps you can keep the

memory alive just by taking a picture of it instead of storing it. The photo acts as your memory trigger and takes up a lot less space in the process. IT REALLY DOES WORK!

11

Place wire shelves in cupboards

Purchase inexpensive wire shelving and you can immediately double your cupboard space. This works well for dishes, glasses, coffee mugs, spices, etc. Use them anywhere you want to maximize shelf space.

12

Put vertical dividers in kitchen cupboards

Vertical dividers are brilliant. Organizing your bakeware upright, rather than having them all piled up on one another, allows easy access to the items you need without having to take everything out of the cupboard first to get to the one you want. The dividers create instant organization at such an inexpensive cost.

13

Use containers to set limits and boundaries

So often people don't pay attention to the space they *really* have available. They figure if their space is full, then they must just need more space. And yes, sometimes that is true.

However, more often than not, what we should be thinking (and what would be painfully clear if we had established limits and boundaries), is that *we just need less stuff.* For instance, I love hair products and they can easily take over my space if my over-consumption isn't reigned in. To keep me in check, I've designated one basket as my limit to the number of hair products I can have. Without that limit, I'm sure my hair products would multiply in the night and take over my entire bathroom. Once the basket is full, I know I have to either stop buying or use the "one in, one out" rule (see Tip 42). These can be tough choices that definitely make me think twice about what I buy in the first place, saving me not only space, but time and money as well.

> **QUICK NOTE:**
> *Use boundaries and limits to keep your consumption in check!*

14

Select containers to create more space

There is just something so rewarding about making *more* fit into a space by using a few carefully selected containers. To me, it's similar to doing a puzzle, trying to arrange and rearrange all the pieces so they fit together just so.

QUICK NOTE:
Storage solutions can help you fit more into the space you have available.

Creative storage solutions can often double the amount of space you currently have and make your home feel larger than it is. For instance, it drives me crazy that there's so much wasted space above the top shelf in a closet. To solve that problem inexpensively, I had my husband add an additional shelf at the top of each of the closets. Then, with the use of

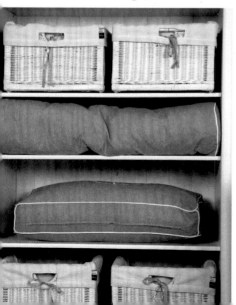

some baskets, I had a place for items I didn't necessarily need daily access to. You may think you don't have enough room to be organized, but with a little creativity, you'll be surprised at the storage you can find.

15

Organizing doesn't have to be expensive— make do

I can definitely understand not being able to organize because you can't seem to find the time, but what I don't understand is not being able to organize because you don't have the money. Please don't let the lack of funds hold you back! We can all dream about having the latest and greatest containers and systems, but what are we to do if our

budget just doesn't allow for us to buy them at this time? It might not be your ideal solution, but something is better than nothing. If you can't afford beautifully lined wicker baskets for your pantry, there is absolutely nothing wrong with purchasing inexpensive Dollar Store baskets to serve the same purpose in the meantime. In fact, even cardboard boxes work well for containing like items together, and they don't cost a penny. Once you have your stuff sorted and purged (which costs you nothing, by the way) *then* contain it any way you can afford, but please don't let not having the money stop you from organizing and appreciating the space you have now.

16

Create a backpack station

I absolutely adore creating stations or zones in my home. Stations serve as a central area for one common task or action, allowing you to save time and, most importantly, your sanity. If you have school-age kids, then you have backpacks to deal with. I recommend having a designated backpack station to keep school stuff contained and organized in one central location. Arrange some hooks by your main entrance for the kids to place their backpacks when they come home from school. In the mornings, the backpacks will be there waiting for them as they rush out the door.

> **QUICK NOTE:**
> *Having defined areas for stuff in your home provides clear direction as to where things belong and need to be stored.*

17

Set up a beverage station

A beverage station creates efficiency in your kitchen by eliminating extra steps spent circling the room for all the items you need at one time. For instance, if while making yourself a pot of tea you have to go to one cupboard for the tea, one cupboard for the pot, another cupboard for the cups, and yet another for the sugar, you're wasting more time than you know. Streamline this process and consolidate all your beverages and beverage supplies into one easy location!

18

Have a donation station

Give your "stuff to go" a temporary home until you can make it to the thrift store. Place a bin or box somewhere in your home to collect these items no longer needed. As you go about your day, get in the habit of asking yourself whether or not an item that you come across can be passed along to someone else. If the answer is yes, you have somewhere to place these items until you have enough to make a trip  to the thrift store. Usually, about once a week, I head out to my local thrift store to empty my box. I like to make a little game out of trying to see how full I can get the box by the end of each week. Trust me, if you're competitive like I am, this challenge is addicting!

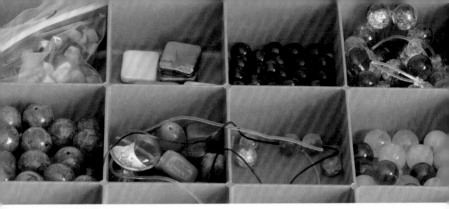

19

Designate a craft center station

If you're a crafter, you don't need me to tell you the amount of stuff that goes along with that title. My goodness, so many bits and pieces! Your time is precious to you and it can cut into valuable crafting time if every time you want to sit down to work on a project it takes a half-hour to collect your supplies. That time-wasting step can be eliminated altogether if you carve out a space to create a craft center station. You may not have a whole room to dedicate to your hobbies, but perhaps you can utilize an old dresser to store items in or a rolling cart that you can move from room to room. And remember, containers help establish limits and boundaries, so having everything in one location like this will prevent you from purchasing excess that only requires more storage space.

20

Create a game station

Do you have games stored all over the house? Be prepared for fun family game nights by storing all your board games in one location. It doesn't have to be fancy. In fact, in our house we use an old garage-sale cabinet to contain all our games in one central location. I use a bin in the cabinet to keep all the cards and smaller games together and multiple shelves hold the larger games. Find what you need when you need it. Are you starting to see a pattern here?

21

Design a gift-wrapping station

Make gift-wrapping easy and enjoyable with a little advance organization. Create a gift-wrap station that contains all the supplies you need for this task. Utilize a dresser, a shelf in a closet, or any of the numerous

QUICK NOTE:
Remember the three C's:
- *Collect supplies.*
- *Consolidate supplies (discard the unused or unwanted items).*
- *Containerize supplies.*

gift-wrap storage solutions on the market today to keep all your necessary items like gift bags, wrap, tape, scissors, bows, cards, and tags all together in one place. This makes it easy to see what you have and what you need and saves time because you don't have to run all over the house looking for everything.

22

Utilize an "I'm outta here" shelf

Without this shelf I would be lost! This is a shelf near my entryway that I use for all the things that don't belong in my house but need to go somewhere else: items that need to  be returned to the store, a friend's plate leftover from the last dinner party, magazines I want to pass along to someone else, letters to be mailed, etc. The trick is to get into two habits: to put stuff on the shelf that has to go out *and* to actually check the shelf before leaving the house to see if there's an errand that can be run on your route. I've made it part of my before bed "ten-minute tidy" to round-up these misplaced items and add them to the shelf so they're ready and waiting for me the next day when I head out to do my errands. (See Tip 35 for details on the "tidy.")

23

Use hooks for kid's coats instead of hangers

Hangers for young kids are a big source of frustration, and hanging something up usually takes more time than little ones care to spend on such a task. Rather than fight my kids day in and day out with the hangers, I put up some hooks instead, and now I'm no longer tripping over dumped coats. Don't set your kids up for failure; create solutions and systems for them that are appropriate for their age level that they can easily manage on their own.

24

Attach hooks on the back of doors for extra storage

Do you have untapped storage potential behind your doors? This often-neglected space is prime real estate for so many different things. Using various-sized hooks, you can hang

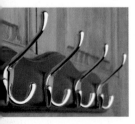

towels, coats, bathrobes, purses, bags, etc. Alternatively, try hanging a shoe organizer on the back of your door to contain anything small, including toys, hats, mitts, socks, or hair supplies. The possibilities are endless. Don't waste this vertical space!

25

Get kids involved with organizing

Organizing is a skill to be taught, practiced, and improved upon like any other, and we aren't doing our kids any favors by not teaching them at a young age. I wouldn't expect my daughter to learn to bake a cake by never allowing her in the kitchen or teaching her how to follow a recipe. Nor will she learn how to organize if I don't teach her the organizing PROCESS and allow her to flex her decision-making muscle.

Since clutter is often defined as decisions we've yet to make, it's important to give kids the opportunity to practice this skill early when the stakes aren't as high. Don't wait until your child isn't home to take over their room and toss what you like. This only creates trust issues and causes them to cling to their stuff even more. Get them involved in the process, teach them to set limits, and allow them to provide input on their space. The outcome may surprise you.

26

Start every week with a menu plan

Menu planning is a wonderful place to start on your organizational journey. It truly has been life-changing for me. I cringe now thinking about all the money we wasted on groceries before menu planning. Saving money is just one of the benefits; there are many more, including healthier eating, saving time, and my all-time favorite, avoiding the 4 p.m. meltdown that occurs when I don't know what to make for dinner. Menu planning involves deciding what you'll eat each day ahead of time, and then only buying the groceries you need for the dishes you have planned. Contrary to popular belief, menu planning is extremely flexible because, even though you may have certain meals scheduled for certain nights, the days can easily be switched around if needed. Since you already have the ingredients, it's so easy to do.

Once a week, sit down with a pad of paper and some recipe books and start slotting in recipes for the week. Keep it simple: The fastest way to failure is to complicate things by picking recipes that are way too time-consuming or elaborate to make. Keep track of recipes you find online in folders on your Internet browser for future reference. Many of my favorite recipes were found on other blogs I read. I really love these recipes because the majority of the time they are tried and true. For more dinner ideas, visit my website and check out Menu Plan Mondays.

27

Set a grocery shopping day and stick to it

One of the keys to my menu planning success is sticking to a set grocery day, which for me is Monday mornings, bright and early. I love going shopping when it's quiet, and I can get in and out without too many hassles. Now grocery shopping day is a habit for me and rarely do I let anything deter me from it.

28

Have a central calendar your whole family can access

This one is important. The key word here is *central*. It's one thing for family members to each have calendars of their own; however, in the name of efficiency, to avoid over-scheduling and scheduling conflicts, it's helpful to have all that information consolidated into one place,

accessible by everyone, including the kids. Ideally, that means one big family calendar as part of your "command center" (see Tip 31). Get in the habit of writing every appointment and event down on this calendar so all members of the family are in the know. If your schedule is really jam-packed, it might even be helpful to take it one step further and color code each person so you can see at a quick glance who needs to be where and when. Additionally, I also recommend taking 20 minutes at the beginning of each year to include the birthdates of friends and family on your central calendar. The fewer places you have to look up information, the more time you'll save, and that means more time for the things you enjoy!

29

Create a visual calendar for young kids

Preschoolers can't read, but they love routine and love to know what's coming next. Create or buy a visual calendar for their level that allows them to see in pictures what they can expect to happen in their day. This helps stop the mental clutter that comes from repeating yourself all day to an inquiring child wanting to know what's ahead for them. It's never too early to introduce daily planning!

QUICK NOTE:
Less chaos and con-fusion results in more time for the things that really matter.

School timetable

Monday	Tuesday	Wednesday	Thursday	Friday	Saturday	Sunday

ABC abc   2+2=4   I luv school

30

If you don't like something, change it or stop complaining

Pay attention to your inner dialogue. When you're dusting your knick-knacks or tripping over your floor clutter and are mumbling and grumbling about it *every* time you do it, you've got to ask yourself if it's really worth it. So often we aren't even conscious of these negative conversations going on in our minds, and it's a lot of mental clutter taking up valuable brain space. Be aware of it, and if it bothers you that much, decide to do something about it—don't keep complaining about it while doing the same things you've always done and expecting different results. It just doesn't work that way. You have the choice to stop letting your clutter control you, or if you choose to do nothing then at least decide to stop contributing to the power of a negative attitude.

QUICK NOTE:
Don't keep repeating the same negative pattern over and over. Do something different.

31

Establish a "command center"

A "command center" is a beautiful thing. It's the ideal spot to capture the bits and pieces of life that are happening right now and can't be filed away just yet. It's not a solution to the permanent filing. Instead, it's a revolving display of miscellaneous documentation, a communication center for the goings-on of life. Perfect for things like important telephone numbers, birthday party invitations, receipts for items needing to be returned, school papers with specific information on an upcoming event, papers that need to be referenced routinely, or bills to be paid. Ideally, you want to choose a central location in your home that you can't help but see every day and that is accessible by all members of the family. It should include a central calendar, a message center, and file holders or bins for each of your children's school papers—and don't forget the chore charts!

32

Re-purpose items for creative storage solutions

Re-purposing a product and using it as a clever storage solution instead is one of my favorite areas of organization. Before I give anything away, I take a look at it and think: *How could I turn this into an organizational tool?* I love the challenge! I've used a beautiful plate rack as a holder for notebooks and then also as a towel holder. Fishing tackle boxes make great toy boxes, especially for tiny pieces. Hairspray caps or baby food jars work great for containing things like push pins and paper-clips. Microwave stands make excellent TV stands or even recycling stations. The list goes on and on. Have fun with it and get creative. WHAT AN INEXPENSIVE WAY TO ORGANIZE!

33

Use labels to know what goes where

Labels serve a great
purpose, especially when
there are multiple people
living in one household.
Labels help everyone know
exactly where something
goes. If you have young
children who can't read
yet, make sure to create
labels with pictures to
help them immediately
recognize what goes
where. Don't have a fancy

label maker? Don't sweat it. You can always print labels out on
your printer using address label sheets or simply make some
using a roll of masking tape and a permanent marker.

34

Color-code the kids

This tip is popular with large families, but it can certainly work no matter what your family size. Color-coding socks, cups, school supplies, towels, and toothbrushes helps reduce disagreements and uncertainly over what belongs to whom. This is a simple solution that packs an organizational punch.

35

Do a "ten-minute tidy" every night before bed

Each night before I go to bed, I do a quick tour of the main floor of my house and perform what I call my "ten-minute tidy." This means I simply ensure everything is tucked back

into its designated space before I go to bed. I also take a moment to check the calendar for scheduling updates and my list notebook (see Tip 47) for any chores and errands that need to be done. It's a positive habit that makes all the difference in my mood the next day. If I'm on top of what needs to be done, I've set myself up to succeed and I can avoid some of the more common pitfalls, including missed appointments, misplaced items, and unhealthy dinners.

36

Mark expiration dates on makeup

The problem we have with sorting through our makeup in order to decide what to keep and what to throw out is *how do we know if it has expired or not*? I solve this problem by keeping a permanent marker in my makeup drawer, along with a list of makeup expiration dates.

Here's a sample of my list:
- Blush and bronzer: *2 years*
- Blush, cream: *12–18 months*
- Concealer: *12–18 months*
- Eye shadow: *powder, 2 years; cream, 12–18 months*
- Eyeliner: *2 years*
- Eyeliner, liquid: *3–6 months*
- Foundation, cream or compact: *18 months*
- Foundation, oil-free: *1 year*
- Fragrance: *18–24 months*
- Lip gloss: *18–24 months*
- Lip liner: *2 years*
- Lipstick: *2 years*
- Mascara: *3 months*
- Moisturizer: *3–12 months*
- Nail color: *1 year*
- Powder: *2 years*

37

Keep flat surfaces clear

Nothing gives you a quicker sense of organization than cleared flat surfaces. It gives you an instant feeling of calm. From dressers to countertops to tables, keep them cleared off! Notice the stuff that continues to get piled up on these surfaces, and find organized storage solutions for it all so your flat surfaces don't continue to be clutter magnets.

38

Work together with a friend for inspiration and motivation

Sometimes it takes fresh eyes to get a new perspective on a space and perhaps some new creative ideas that you may have overlooked. The right friend will also help you stay on task. Another option is to consider hiring a professional organizer.

To find a professional organizer in your area, contact one of the following national organizations:

National Association of Professional Organizers:

www.napo.net

Professional Organizers in Canada:

www.organizersincanada.com

39

Don't keep out-of-season clothes in prime real estate space

If you've got a limited amount of space in your closet, you may want to consider storing your out-of-season clothing in another location to free up easily accessible space in your closet. I don't know about you, but I get depressed in the winter if I open my closet and see tank tops taunt me for warmer days. So for that reason, and in an effort to make my closet space function as efficiently as possible, I use three designated shelves in the middle of my closet to act as seasonal

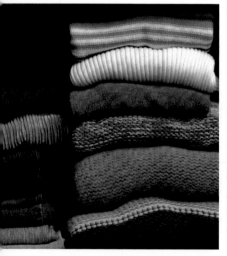

storage switch-out locations. For instance, at the beginning of winter I remove all my shorts and tank tops from these shelves and move them to clear totes underneath my bed. Long-sleeve shirts and fleece pants take over this coveted position so they're readily available to me during the colder months.

40

Purge clothing at the end of the season, not the beginning

Purging clothes at the end of the season rather than the beginning makes sense because what you've worn and not worn over the course of the season is still fresh in your memory. If you didn't wear it this season, chances are very good you won't next year, either. It's time to let it go. Go through each piece with a critical eye and ask yourself some key questions to help you decide.

41

Learn these eleven tips for parting with your clothes

1. If you haven't worn something in a year, then out it goes, regardless of condition, price, or size. A year works because you cover every season in that period of time. If you haven't worn it during the year, you probably never will.

2. If you have a piece of clothing that you wear, but are annoyed with it every time you do, stop wearing it!

3. If it's waiting to be mended and it's been waiting for a long time, then enough is enough! Get rid of it.

4. If you hate to iron and your ironing pile sits there neglected while you wear your favorite clothing over and over again, why do you still have an ironing pile?

5. I'm not opposed to keeping your "skinny" clothes (and I know we all do it), but, for goodness sakes, you don't need to keep all of it! Styles change, your tastes change, your body shape changes, so chances are good that when you get back to that size, you're going to want new stuff, anyway.

6   If you absolutely love a shirt, but never wear it because you have nothing to wear it with, well guess what—a mate isn't going to magically appear! Follow the one-year rule.

7   Sentimental clothes that you aren't wearing shouldn't reside in your closet. Either take a picture of it and preserve the memory, or limit yourself to one tote of "clothes to show my kids so they can laugh their heads off at me someday."

8   Don't hang on to something that is "just all right" because you don't have something better yet to replace it with. Let it go now.

9   You don't have to do it all at once. Try purging in stages and be motivated by your success. One day you could do shirts, the next day shorts, etc.

10 Try everything on. This one I can't stress enough. Do not hold something up and think, "Oh, this is so beautiful, I'm going to keep it." That's too easy, and what you might not remember is that, although it's beautiful, the buttons gape at the front revealing enough cleavage to make you blush! Get rid of it.

11 You only have the space that you do. Jamming your clothes into the closet and fighting with them every single day to find what you need won't make your closet grow in the night. It will only make you grumpy. It's not worth it.

42

Use the "one in, one out" rule

You've probably heard this classic organizational tip over and over again, but it's too good not to include in a book about conquering clutter. The idea is that for every new thing you bring into the house, one must go out. It works really well with clothes, but of course also works for just about everything else, too. Practice this rule on a regular basis and you'll kick clutter to the curb once and for all.

43

Keep toy sets together in specific rooms

Toys can easily take over the house if you aren't careful. One of the tricks that helped in my home is to keep toy sets (dolls,

QUICK NOTE: *Toys should not only be assigned to specific rooms, but also have designated spaces within that room. This makes clean-up a whole lot easier.*

cars, action figures, etc.) together in specific rooms. It's such a small thing, but you would not believe how much easier it makes life. After much training, even my two-year-old has it figured out. For instance, his little tool bench and tools are kept upstairs in his bedroom, and whenever he'd come downstairs with one of his tools in his chubby little hand, I'd send him right back upstairs to put it back. He actually caught on pretty quickly. While everything isn't always put away exactly, toy sets are at least all together in the same room, which is nice when you want to sit down to play something and you don't have to go looking all over the house for the pieces.

44

Use toy boxes only for large items

I'm not a huge fan of toy boxes because they end up becoming the bottomless pit. They work nicely for large baby toys, but as soon as the children grow and the toys get smaller, different storage solutions work better. Some of my favorites include bookshelves with baskets, cubbies with bins, clear shoe box containers, and rolling carts with drawers. Short on floor space? Try moving the dresser into the closet. Another space-saver in our home: using big, clear bins underneath the bed for my son's Legos. He can easily slide them out when he wants to play with them and back in when it's time to clean up.

45

Schedule regular toy "clean-outs"

In order to avoid toys overwhelming your home, get in the habit of weeding out the toys just before birthdays and holidays. Make a date with the kids to tackle the toys a couple of weeks before these big events. Kids tend to be more on board with this idea knowing that more toys are right around the corner. Remove toys from all

QUICK NOTE: *Remember, your favorites don't need to be their favorites.*

surfaces, drawers, toy boxes, and closets. Get the kids involved sorting like with like, and then move on to purging all items that are missing pieces, outgrown, or in excess. Ask your child direct questions such as: When did you play with this last? Do you think some other child might like to play with this now? Which one of these is your favorite? and, Would you like to keep this one or this one?

46

Toss your junk mail right away

As soon as you touch your mail, do a quick sort and immediately throw out the junk rather than let it pile up. Drop it right into the trash basket or recycling. Have a designated spot for your bills and put bills that come in directly there. Create a home for items that come in, such as those that need to be actioned, papers that need to be referenced regularly, schedules, and upcoming events to keep them from spreading out all over your kitchen countertops.

Two of my favorite storage methods for actionable and important papers are desktop file holders or, if flat surfaces are at a premium, the Fridge File, which is a magnetic pocket filing system for your fridge.

47

Utilize notebooks and lists

Use a notebook to keep track of detailed lists. Rather than have Post-it Notes and little scraps of paper all over the house, try containing your to-do lists into one lined notebook. Start by writing the date at the top of the page, and then write down every single  task that's taking up more space than it needs to in your head. Listing your tasks individually instead of listing whole projects will help you batch and consolidate tasks based on what needs to be done, saving you all sorts of time, energy, and money. For example, if you want to make year-end teacher gifts, list all the steps associated with this particular project rather than listing only the project itself. Steps might include buying craft supplies, making cards, making the craft, and buying the packaging. Similarly, batching all your errands will save you from making multiple trips. Or, if after reviewing your detailed list you see that you have multiple phone calls to make, you can clear a space in your day to make them all at once.

48

Set your daily top-three to-dos

While I think it's a great idea to have a running list of all the tasks needed to be completed, I also know it can be so easy for our day to get away from us and feel like nothing was accomplished. That's why I always recommend taking a couple of minutes each morning to select, from your notebook list, your top three to-dos for the day. Concentrate on those three things first and determine to get them done. That way, no matter what else happens during the day, you can go to bed at night knowing that you hit your target and can feel good about what you've accomplished.

49

Don't look up

Sometimes the mountain of a task in front of us can seem so overwhelming that we simply drag our feet and do nothing. We look around at our spaces and think: *I'm never going to get to the end*. It's frustrating and draining when the task ahead seems to be more than we can handle. Don't let the "mountain" keep you from taking the necessary steps to move forward. Don't look ahead. Instead, keep your eyes down, only focusing on the task at hand. If you have a room that you want to organize, start with a drawer, move to the next drawer, and work your way around the room one tiny step at a time. Keep moving, and before you know it, you'll be at the top of the mountain giving yourself a pat on the back. You'll look back on the path you traveled and feel mighty proud of yourself. AND SO YOU SHOULD!

50

If you haven't used something in a year, get rid of it

Another fantastic organizing rule that keeps clutter from taking over your life is the "one-year rule." If you haven't used something over the period of one year, get rid of it. This

QUICK NOTE:
Ask yourself: Do you want to live in a home or a storage locker?

rule doesn't so much pertain to the sentimental stuff (there's a whole other rule for that!—see Tip 10), but instead to the stuff that is lying around your home, taking up valuable space that isn't being used. Toys, sports equipment, small appliances, shoes, clothes, blankets, tools, vases, games, decorations, crafts, and so much more. If you have the space and it's not bothering anyone, then by all means store it—but the fact that you've picked up this book in the first place leads me to believe you might need help with your clutter. If you're not sure if you've used something in a year or not, then right now go around your home and storage areas and put small dot stickers or Post-it Notes on items you're unsure of. Write the date on your calendar. As you use something, remove the sticker and carry on. At the end of the year, anything still

wearing a dot or Post-it is out the door.

51

If it doesn't fit the vision for the space, get rid of it

The first step to the organizing PROCESS is to Plan. Plan what you want for the space and how you want it to function and serve you. That's right, if your craft room is now a big storage room of stuff that hasn't seen the light of day in years, then your space is no longer serving you as effectively as it could. Yes, you may need additional storage space, but at what cost? Think about what you're giving up now to store this stuff for later.

52

Keep a wastebasket in every room

To cut down on clutter and keep the garbage from piling up, make it easy for your kids to throw stuff out. Supply each room with a wastebasket to make tidying up quick and easy. Line each basket with a grocery bag, and once a week assign a child to go around to each room to collect the trash and replace the bags. This is a great chore for younger kids.

53

Cut the knick-knacks out

I always think that anyone with a lot of knick-knacks in their home must love dusting. To me, fewer trinkets means less work. Have you really looked around your home lately? Do you feel the need to fill every nook

and cranny with a little of this and a little of that? I'm not opposed to decorations, but if you aren't using something and it isn't bringing a smile to your face every time you see or use it, why are you hanging onto it? *Remember: Flat surfaces have a calming effect and cluttered surfaces are chaotic, mentally*

and physically. You may not even realize it now, but you certainly will once you lighten the load of the space. Give yourself permission to *only* surround yourself with the things that bring you joy and provide you with order, function, and efficiency on a regular basis. So what do you say, could it be time to part with a few things?

54

Set your own clutter standards

Your clutter standards are your level of "good enough." Are you setting the bar too high or too low? Too high, and you may be setting yourself up for failure with standards that are impossible to maintain on a regular basis. Too low, and your family may be struggling with chaos on a regular basis. Only

you can decide where the middle ground is for your family. Are you constantly looking for things, tripping over your clutter, paying bills late, perpetually late for appointments, and living in chaos? Is it stressing you out? Then it's time to be organized enough to avoid the things that stress you the most without setting yourself up for failure. For instance, I don't make my kids clean up their rooms every night before bed, but I do expect them to leave a path to the bed. That's good enough for me. Give it some thought and decide what's good enough for you.

55

Store stuff where you use it

It only makes sense that if you put your makeup on at the kitchen table every day (and some do!), you can save yourself precious morning minutes by coming up with an inconspicuous storage solution that allows you to keep it where you'll need it. Don't make things more complicated than they need to be. Store stuff where you use it and you'll save yourself unnecessary steps and stress. If your kids like to do art at the table while you're cooking dinner each night, then make it easier for them by creating an art station you can keep right in your dining room. If your husband drops his clothes beside the bed every night instead of the hamper in

the closet, then consider moving the hamper to beside the bed. It might not always be the logical place to store something, but if it works for you and reduces your stress, then it's worth considering the change.

56

Use memory binders or totes to organize kids' keepsakes

My technique for keeping special school papers and artwork organized is to use memory binders. I have a different binder for each child and store each year in clear page-protector sheets. These binders are kept easily accessible in my office, and throughout the year I can very quickly just put the special papers/awards/notes/ stories that they want to keep right into their binder. Having one page-protector sheet per school year really forces us  to put limits on what we keep. I don't want to burden my kids with excess when they're grown. I always ask myself, "Is this my memory or theirs?" What we hang on to is what is important to them, not me. Sure, I help guide them with their decision making if they need it, but ultimately keeping what is of most value to them is what is most important to me. For any larger keepsake items (special outfits, baby books, journals, art, etc.), I keep one clear tote for each child in their closet. This provides an excellent limit to the number of items that can be saved.

57

Do not keep more than three months' backlog of magazine articles

I love magazines. I love to flip through them and get immersed in the colors and sights of possibilities. Unfortunately, they too can pile up and taunt us with another item left undone on our to-do list. If your pile surpasses three months of magazines, it's time to cut your losses. Three months is a good rule of thumb, and anything older than that should be passed on to someone else to enjoy.

58

Keep manuals with the receipt stapled to them all in one place

Purchase an inexpensive file tote from any department store or make room in the filing cabinet you have for warranties and manuals. As soon as you purchase a new big-ticket item, immediately staple the receipt to the manual and file it away. I take it one step further and file the manuals by item type (vacuum under V, for instance), but what you do will depend on your clutter standard. This allows you to have all the information you need right at your fingertips if you need to make a return or reference a manual.

59

Pack activity bags

I like to be prepared for spontaneity. In other words, I like
to keep packed activity bags for various excursions so that
if an unexpected opportunity arises, we're ready to go! For
example, in the summer I keep a packed beach bag right in
the back of the van that includes sunscreen, towels, hats, and
beach toys. You never know when it's going to be a great day
for the beach! If your children are in sports activities, keep
their equipment bags packed and ready to go by the door.
This makes them quick and easy to grab when you need to.
Just remember to restock after you use them!

60

Keep your vehicle stocked with essentials

You never know what's going to happen when you're out and about. Organization helps you be prepared for what life throws at you. While we can't control the traffic, weather, or even sick kids, we *can* keep our vehicles stocked to help us in these situations should they happen. Grab yourself a container and fill it with a first aid kit, wipes, a change of clothes if you have little ones, extra diapers, Ziploc bags for travel sickness, tissues, receiving blankets (these work at any age for quick cleanups!), activity kits for traffic-stalling boredom, and of course, snacks and water. Don't forget to keep a trash bag in your car at all times as well. You wouldn't throw garbage on your floor at home, so don't do it in the vehicle, either. Every time you get gas, get in the habit of dumping the garbage. Just a little advance planning can make a *huge* difference to how your day will end up playing out.

61

Use a purse organizer or clear bags to organize your purse or bag

My purse organizer changed my life. It is by far one of my most favorite containers. I highly recommend a purse organizer inside your handbag to keep track of all your essentials. There are many on the market, but my favorite is the Purse Perfector for its durability and functionality. It makes all the difference in the world to not have to waste time searching through your bag for a pen, a stick of gum, or your cell phone. Everything will be tucked in and looking pretty in their special little slots. Clear sandwich bags also work nicely to keep items contained so you can find what you need when you need it. DOESN'T THAT SOUND WONDERFUL?

62

Embrace Plan B and let go of perfectionism

Have you ever been consumed by the thought that if you can't do something perfectly, why do it at all? Or, life as you know it will certainly fall apart if things don't go according to your plan? Do you agonize over every mistake you make? Are your expectations of yourself and others so high that no one can ever live up to them, leaving you and those around you overwhelmed and frustrated? What I've discovered in my journey is that I don't need to be afraid of going to Plan B. In fact, Plan B is often a much better option if I'm open to the possibilities. I may even have to go to plan D or Q, but you know what? It isn't the end of the world. What it allows me to do is live more in the present because I'm not dwelling on what I really have no control  of, anyway. I've discovered that I actually love the challenge of switching into Plan B mode. Instead of panicking, I immediately say to myself, "Okay, we're going to Plan B— how can I make the most of this situation?" I like this problem-solving mode. It's a challenge, a new way of looking at things, and as a result, a new, more relaxed, me. For example, last Christmas, when my turkey was two hours late in cooking, I didn't go into a tailspin meltdown as I may have done in previous years. Instead, I served up some cheese and crackers, pulled out some board games, and had a great time with my guests! And it wasn't the end of the world.

63

Keep projects in progress under control

Projects in progress can hold us back, whether we're aware of it or not. Do you have projects that don't interest you anymore, that have been cluttering up your space for years, yet you feel some sort of obligation to complete? It might be time to let them go and feel the weight lift from your shoulders as a result. Go ahead, what are you waiting for? Think about whether or not the space you have given your clutter permission to take over could be put to better use. Are you *really* willing to give up square footage of usable space in your home for stuff you "might" just use or need one day? Really stop and think about the power you're putting in your clutter's hands. What kind of hold does it have on you and why are you allowing it to happen?

64

Disguise your storage

Magazines and remotes scattered all over the coffee table look like clutter, as do toys piled in the middle of the floor. Try storing them in such a way as to disguise the clutter. For instance, use a storage ottoman or a basket underneath your coffee table to store all those toys in your living room. Pretty baskets also work great to control all those magazines and remotes. Giving them a home may not keep them from getting scattered all over the place, but it certainly does make cleanup a breeze, and it helps with setting limits.

65

Use rolling plastic drawer units

I absolutely love the plastic drawer units on wheels. They aren't the most attractive things on the block, but boy are they an organizational gem at an inexpensive price. Add some baskets inside the drawers and your organizational high will

be off the charts! Use these to create a craft or art zone for your kids, a homework caddy, or even Lego storage. These also work wonderfully for additional storage in closets.

66

Implement a weekly cleaning schedule

I worked full-time when my oldest two were little. I look back on that period now and wonder how I ever did it. I do remember it being stressful, but with the exception of having housecleaning help (I was fortunate to be able to hire a house cleaner every two weeks), I still managed to get everything else done. When I first came home, I couldn't figure out why I struggled with getting everything done, considering I now had more time in the day to do it. I was really overwhelmed by it all. That's when I realized it was because I was no longer following any sort of schedule. I fell into the trap that I had nothing *but* time now that I was home. I told myself that there was always tomorrow, or the next day, or the day after that. The longer I procrastinated, the more stressed I was; the more stressed I was, the more chaotic my household was. So, as a family, we sat down and created a weekly chore schedule. We made a list of all the chores that needed to be performed, assigning them to a specific day and person. Of course, there are still some days that I get off track, but having my schedule written out and posted where I see it regularly helps to remind me of what I need to do and when. Knowing that I don't have to commit any more than an hour to housecleaning each day helps me to stay focused and get it done. Talk about freeing! Whether you're a stay-at-home mom or a work-from-home mom or you work outside of the home, *committing* to a schedule and following through will help you achieve whatever goal you're seeking for yourself and your family. TRY IT!

67

Create a "Housekeeping Mission Statement"

Having a "Housekeeping Mission Statement" is a daily reminder of what my goals are for my family and home. It's so easy to lose sight of what's truly important in our day-to-day lives, and having a mission statement

posted where I can see it helps me stay focused and on track. I'm amazed at what a difference it makes in my attitude.

My Housekeeping Mission Statement:

To provide an inviting and peaceful household environment for my family and all who enter that is conducive to living simply, loving deeply, and laughing abundantly. I will make strides everyday to achieve this by practicing and teaching good daily habits and routines, along with effective organizational skills. I will graciously and cheerfully serve my family and genuinely enjoy my commitment to creating a home sanctuary that is, above all else, pleasing to God.

68

Have a handy library basket

All library books coming into the house that must eventually go back out are kept in a designated library basket in the living room. The kids can each take one book at a time out of the basket, and as soon as they're finished with it, they are to put it back into the basket. This keeps the books all in one place, and when we're heading out the door to go to the library, it's easy to round up all the books. The other library rule that helps to further enforce the use of the basket is that the kids are responsible for any library fines on the books they take out. What a difference it makes when it's *their* money on the line!

69

Limit your family to two towels and two sets of sheets per person

I think sometimes we get carried away with our collections of sheets and towels, and our linen closets are bursting at the

seams as a result. My rule: two sets of each per person, plus one set for guests. I find that having one set for each bed and another to replace it with on wash day is

more than enough. Towels also don't need to be changed every day, considering we're clean when we dry ourselves with them. Just make sure that you hang them up to dry properly so they don't smell. And just think, simplifying your linen closet will free up all sorts of space that can be used for other storage needs.

70

Use space bags

If you have a really small linen closet or no hall closet at all, space bags are an excellent way to take big, bulky items and shrink them down to fit smaller spaces. These can now be purchased fairly inexpensively at most department stores. They are reusable and air- and water-tight, protecting the contents from dirt, bugs, mildew, and odors. They're also great for storing patio cushions during the winter!

71

Utilize online photo books for pictures

Pictures can be one of the hardest things to stay on top of. We get them downloaded onto our computers, but then what? Printing your favorites is an option, but then you've got to put them somewhere, and all those photo albums can take up an awful lot of space. My suggestion is to switch to photo books. Photo books are an online version of scrapbooking that can be created quickly and easily online, and the printed albums are so thin that they take up no space at all. Print books by year, by child, or by event—whatever works for you. There's also have a journaling option that allows you to record any meaningful tidbits you don't want to forget. There are many different online photo book websites to choose from including a couple of my personal favorites, Shutterfly and Inkubook.

72

Create a "to file" basket

I really hate filing and I have a tendency to let it pile up. Perhaps you can relate. To keep my pile from getting out of hand, I use a basket on top of my filing cabinet to set my limit. Once the basket is full, I know it's time to file. This is one of the clutter standards that works for me.

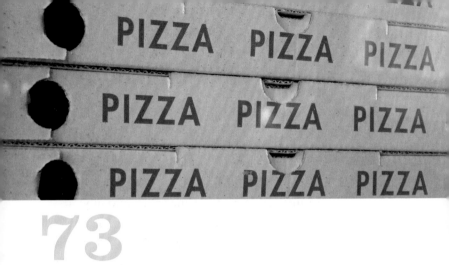

73

Use pizza boxes for scrapbook paper or children's artwork

Inexpensive storage solutions are my favorite ones! A neat storage solution for scrapbook paper is to use large pizza boxes. The paper fits perfectly and the boxes stack beautifully. Check with your local pizza place.

74

Use visual cues to eliminate clutter.

Sometimes with everything else going on, we can't remember what we've used and what we haven't. It's time for some visual cues. For instance, turn the hangers around in your closet to face the opposite direction; as you wear something, turn the hanger back around. At the end of the season, you'll know exactly what you've worn and what needs to be purged. Alternatively, place small stickers on your clothing, and when

you wear something, remove the sticker. Anything remaining with a sticker after a year is ready to leave the nest.

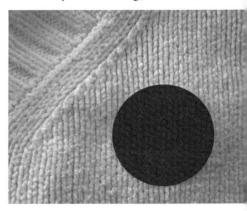

75

Install closet organizers

....

Closets without organizers seem naked and are crying out
for organization. You can literally double the amount of
closet space you have by adding an organizer to it, and I'm
not talking an expensive one, either. You can get perfectly
wonderful *inexpensive* closet organizers at most department
stores. I like the ones that provide the cubbies in the middle—
they make my heart sing!

76

Create a binder and online folder for recipes

Do you collect recipes, but then never reference them because it's too overwhelming to even think about sorting through them all? I wouldn't call this a collection, I would call it clutter. A pile of stuff you aren't using. If the idea of trying to organize it stresses you out even more, then you might want to consider just purging the stack altogether. However, if you really do want to keep them all to use one day (be honest with yourself here), then a better system is definitely in order. I limit myself to two binders total to contain the recipes my family loves, and I have tab dividers based on the meal type (chicken, beef, breakfasts, soup, etc). To save paper, I try not to print recipes anymore. I simply bring my laptop to the kitchen and cook dinner right there. If a recipe

is a keeper, I add it to my "Family Favorites Recipes" index on my website. When I find recipes online that I want to try, I save them in a recipes folder in my bookmarks tab. That main folder then has additional folders similar to the tab dividers I have in my recipe binders. This system makes it very quick and easy to add to my weekly menu plan.

77

Use drawer dividers

A drawer without a divider is a big jumbled mess. All it takes are a few good containers to make even a junk drawer look good. Inexpensive Dollar Store baskets fit the bill here perfectly because they come in all different sizes and shapes. Mix and match to get the fit you need. Use them to sort everything from stationery supplies, to socks and underwear, and instantly feel a "high" from the organization you've just created in a short amount of time. Trust me, you'll want more.

> QUICK NOTE: *Tea, tissue, cracker, and cereal boxes all work well as drawer dividers. Simply cut off the top flaps and cut them down to the size you need. Fabulously inexpensive!*

Designate a charging station

Is your home overrun with chargers for cell phones, music, and gaming devices? Set up a "one-stop charging station" in your home that makes it easy for family members to connect their electronics to in order to charge them. Charging stations can now be purchased inexpensively and serve to contain all

 these devices in one area and make them easily accessible. You can also make a charging station yourself by drilling a hole in the back of a cabinet or drawer large enough to feed a power cord into, and then tucking these gadgets into the drawer to keep surface clutter to a minimum.

79

Make a jewelry organizer

Create your own jewelry organizer by taking a ribbon memo board and adding some small hooks to it, about two or three inches apart. Your jewelry won't get tangled, and with it easily accessible like this, you'll remember exactly what you own so all pieces will get worn. BEAUTIFUL!

80

Think about your habits

A lot of what I'm talking about in this book isn't directly related to the stuff that clutters up our lives, but the *habits* that are responsible for the clutter in the first place. The clutter will continue to accumulate if we don't break free of the habitual actions that hold us captive to it.

We can go through the PROCESS over and over again without new results if we don't make the necessary habit adjustments that are required to make the systems work. For instance, creating a command center and having a home for all those really important papers still doesn't mean those papers will just magically know to walk themselves there.

> QUICK NOTE: *No carefully constructed system is going to work without some carefully disciplined habits to match.*

There is *action* to be taken on your part to make it work. You may find your system to be too complicated at first or it may need to be simplified. Before tossing it out altogether, consider whether or not you've given the system a fair trial, which is about three weeks. I'm betting that once you replace your old habit of just dumping those papers on your kitchen counter and tucking them into their new special homes instead, you'll be doing a happy dance when you need something and—lo and behold—you find it in a minute or less. SUPER YAY!

81

Label the lids of spices

Remember I told you I didn't alphabetized my spices? That's true, I don't, but I do have the lids all labeled. Let me explain. To maximize efficiency in your kitchen, try keeping your spices in a shallow basket in your

QUICK TIP:
Keep your baking and cooking spices in separate baskets, which makes it faster to find what you need.

lazy Susan. The basket works to contain them and keeps them from taking over the space entirely. Labeling the lids of each spice jar means that every time you open the cabinet and look down, you can immediately see what you have and go right for the one you need. Since I don't have many spices that I use regularly, I didn't find it necessary to take it that one step further to alphabetize; however, you can easily incorporate this step if it means it will save you some stress and make a difference in your day. GO FOR IT!

82

Make a rule: no food in bedrooms

You know what comes with food? Empty dishes and garbage
that not only contributes to the clutter of the room, but
to the mess that results when things get spilled. I solved
this problem by eliminating food and drinks in bedrooms
altogether. If someone wants something to eat, they
come down to the kitchen and get it. They spend time
with their family socializing while they do so. WORKS
BEAUTIFULLY!

83

Use a system to organize kid clothes

The system I use in my home for organizing kid clothes is this: everything currently being worn lives in a dresser with one drawer for socks/underwear/PJs, one drawer for shirts,

one drawer for pants, and, depending on the season, one for shorts and/or sweaters. My daughter's dresses hang in the closet. The next size to grow into hangs in the closet, ready to go. Bigger sizes after that live in totes or a toy box in a closet. Yes that's right, a toy box. Remember I told you I wasn't a fan of the toy box for smaller toys? Well, when you can't use a product for its original purpose, re-use it for something else! The reason I prefer the dresser for current clothes is because it makes it quick and easy for the kids to maintain and that saves this momma a lot of time.

84

Tackle small tasks to get big results

So often we don't want to start an organizing project because we think it will take too long. Trying to find large chunks of time can seem overwhelming. Thankfully, many organizing tasks can be completed in short bursts of attention. Committing to these small tasks on a daily basis creates a sense of accomplishment that fuels continuation and fosters self-discipline. Once you see how easy and rewarding it is to tackle one small task or space at a time, the impact of those results will make you want to do it over and over and over again...until you become an addict like me!

Organizing tasks that can be done in 30 minutes or less:

- Organize a drawer
- Organize a bookshelf
- File papers
- Update your calendar
- Organize DVDs
- Check for expired products in your fridge
- Sort hats and mitts
- Create e-mail folders (see Tip 90)
- Organize your wallet or purse
- Clean out backpacks
- Tidy your desk

85

Regularly go through the medicine cabinet for expired products

If you're a parent, I'm sure you've been through this scenario: Your child comes down with a cold in the middle of the night and you head to the medicine cabinet, only to find it empty or the products you do have expired. Not fun! To keep this from happening, I suggest keeping your medications and vitamins in a basket in a kitchen cupboard.

That way, whenever you're waiting on supper to cook or water to boil, it's quick and easy to pull down the basket to do a periodic check of what needs to be refilled. Don't be caught without again!

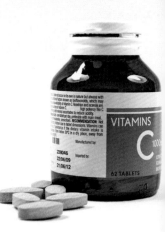

86

Stop sorting your laundry

Let's face it: Laundry
is a never-ending task.
It was for me as well,
until I eliminated the
entire sorting process
altogether. Oh, yes I
did! In fact, sorting
clothes is highly
overrated. Instead, I

keep a laundry basket in each child's room, and when their
basket is full, I throw the entire load into the washer *without*
separating the whites and colors...gasp! Can you believe
it? I certainly couldn't! I thought for sure the colors would
run, but they didn't. In fact, the laundry came out just fine.
Adding about a ½ cup of vinegar to each load helps set the
colors and keep them from running. (Caution: Always wash
new red items or dark denim separately the first time.) I've yet
to wreck a piece of clothing doing it this way, and because I'm
only washing one child's clothes at a time, I no longer waste
any time trying to figure out whose socks are whose. LIFE
CHANGING!

87

Organize coupons

Coupons are only worth something if you remember to take them with you to the store. This is often where many people get hung up. Others get overwhelmed with not knowing how to organize them all so that when they do go to the store they can quickly find what they need. If coupons are a problem for you, and you'd

QUICK COUPON TIPS:

QUICK COUPON TIPS:
- Set aside some additional time each week while planning your weekly menu to cut applicable coupons.
- Use a binder with clear plastic baseball-sheet inserts or a small accordion file to organize your coupons. Categorize them by product type or alphabetize them by product name.
- Keep coupons in your vehicle along with your recyclable bags, or keep them right in your purse in order to always have them available.

really like to take advantage of them more, then figure out where your roadblock is. Is it finding them, cutting them out, organizing them, or just not having them with you when you shop? Be realistic about the time you have available to devote to this task, and incorporate a system that works within that boundary. Decide what action(s) you can put into place today to make that system work. Unrealistic expectations only set you up for failure.

88

Streamline kitchen utensils

If you're short on drawer space, store your cooking utensils near the stove in a container big enough for all your storage needs. My favorite is the Pampered Chef Turnabout because it easily turns so you can access all sides and it's big enough to hold everything you need. This serves as a great limit to the number of utensils you can have. If you have too many utensils and are having trouble parting with any of them, follow Organizing Guru Peter Walsh's great one-month cardboard-box tip: Dump all your utensils into a box and as you use them, put them back into the kitchen drawer or organizer. Anything still left in the box after a month, except maybe a couple of utensils you might only use on special occasions, gets tossed. No excuses!

89

Organize your pantry

Pantries can easily get out of control because in an effort to get in and out quickly, we just toss stuff in. Problem is, then we forget what we have and just continue to buy more. More stuff just exacerbates the problem, making it that much more overwhelming to deal with. Now is the time to tackle it by following the PROCESS steps mentioned at the beginning of this book. Your plan is to have an organized space so finding what you need can be done instantly. Start by removing every single last item; stack it all up on the dining room table. This sounds like it's going to take a long time, but I promise you it won't. Then, sort it all out into categories (tomato sauces, cans of beans, sauce packets, etc.). Throw out all the expired products. Now create a section for everything. Use shelf dividers if necessary to help you create some boundaries. Keep like items together and add labels to each section to help all family members know where everything goes. Remove granola bars and other snacks from their cardboard packaging and dump them all into one big snack basket for easy access (see Tip 3).

90

Create an e-mail folder system

E-mail can get out of hand quickly, if we aren't careful. Eventually, they all just pile up on one another until we can't find what we need. It's really no different than paper piles. While it may not be physical clutter that we're tripping over, if it causes us frustration or stress, then it's still clutter. Here are my suggestions: Every time you log into your e-mail, the first thing you should do is purge the junk. Delete it immediately. What should be left are e-mails that need to be referenced or actioned. Create file folders with easily

identifiable titles and file your e-mails away in the appropriate folder so you'll be able to find what you need quickly and easily. The only e-mails I leave in my inbox are those that require an action. I use this as my to-do list, although you could create a folder for those as well. If you find that you never bother to read your subscription e-mails, be honest about it and unsubscribe from them. This "just in case" pattern with e-mails is no different from our physical clutter. Decide right now what is a priority for you, and move forward with a clean slate.

91

Cut the clutter in your bedroom and create the sanctuary you deserve

While our kitchens may be the hub of our homes, our bedrooms should be places we come to unwind and relax, and eventually sleep, after a long day. Yet, why is it that the master bedroom so often gets neglected? It can quickly become a dumping ground, the surfaces piled high with clutter and clothes. Maybe it's because it isn't generally a room guests see, so it's easy to throw things in and quickly shut the door, or maybe it's just last on the list because so many other areas in the house need tending to first. A cluttered bedroom is a chaotic one, opposite of the calm it should be and a constant reminder of things left undone. It isn't so easy to turn that off at night when it's all around you. If you're having trouble sleeping at night, it could be the clutter piled up around you. Don't neglect this area—find homes for the stuff that doesn't belong and get it out. After all, it's your bedroom, not a storage locker. As you close your eyes at the end of the day, you'll be glad you did.

92

Invite company over as motivation

Need to do a whole house clutter bust? Invite company over. Many of us work better with a deadline, so invite someone over who has never seen the place before and will want the grand tour. WORKS EVERY TIME!

93

Use binder clips for cables

Today, so many devices in the home need to be charged with a USB cable. From MP3 devices to cameras, these cords can quickly get out of hand. A simple solution for all those cables is to attach some binder clips to the side of your desk without closing the clips. Slide each cord through the end of the clip and let them dangle untangled at the side of the desk ready and waiting for quick recharges. Don't forget to label each cord!

94

Use Command Hooks to save space

I hate wasting any square inch of space in my home. I like to put it all to good use, but because I tend to arrange and then rearrange things on a regular basis, I do like storage solutions that aren't permanent. That's the beauty of 3M Command Hooks. These are an absolute essential item in my organizational tool kit. Designed to hold various weights and to suit various decor needs, these hooks can be placed anywhere in your home, and can be removed with a simple pull, all without doing any damage to your walls. Use them anywhere in your home you need a hook: behind doors, in closets to hold purses and scarves, in the kitchen for hot mitts and aprons, or by the front door for keys and backpacks. Change your mind or time for a change? No problem. Simply pull straight down on the adhesive and the hook pops right off. ABSOLUTELY BRILLIANT!

95

Keep toothbrushes organized

Eliminate toothbrush confusion by giving each family member their own small container in a drawer to keep both their toothbrush and their own toothpaste organized. Not only does this eliminate fighting between siblings but it's an easy system for little ones to maintain.

96

Use camera bags for video games

Want to keep all of your child's video game equipment contained and organized? Head to your local thrift shop and pick up a used camera bag. Most come with all sorts of pockets, padding, and zippers, and are absolutely ideal for this purpose. Put a Command Hook behind your child's door or in a central location, and you won't have to worry about where all the accessories and games have gone. Also perfect to grab and go for traveling!

97

Don't put it off until later

Every time we handle something in our home, we have to make a decision about it: Where do I put it? Should I toss it, file it, store it, or hide it? Unfortunately, the more popular choice—and one that most often leads to clutter problems—is deciding not to do anything at  all. (And yes, that still counts as a decision made.) However, deciding not to do anything at all doesn't make the item go away, and instead it becomes the start of yet another pile to be dealt with later. Start handling incoming items (toys, paper, clothes, etc.) immediately by making a decision about what to do with it that doesn't involve doing nothing at all. Of course, flexing this decision-making muscle gets easier with practice, so start small and work your way up. And remember, decisions can be made faster when there's a designated home for everything and organized systems already in place. You'll immediately know where something goes and can put it right there. DON'T DELAY, PUT IT AWAY TODAY!

98

Organize your entryway

The entryway is the first room you see when you come into your home, and whether you have a big space or one on the smaller side, you're sending a message to everyone who enters (including yourself) about the nature of your home. When you walk in your front door, does it say *welcome* to those who enter? Do you see a chaotic scene with shoes and coats thrown about? Do you find yourself tensing up as you maneuver your way around obstacles dropped at the door? Our entryways need to work extra hard for us, and it will take a little creativity to maximize space in this area. If floor space is at a premium, consider going vertical with shelves, using the back of the door for storage and adding a closet organizer to the closet. Pay attention to the items landing on the floor, and figure out where you can designate a home for them. Give each child their own basket or bin to store hats, mitts, sunglasses, etc. My number-one space-saving tip in this area of the house is to switch out your coats and accessories with the seasons. Store the seasonal clothing in labeled bins in another area of your home or garage.

99

Focus!

One of the fastest ways to jeopardize an organizing project is to get distracted by the things you're trying to sort through. For instance, you want to organize your office, but get completely sidetracked looking at old yearbooks, or you sit down to organize your photos and can't get help but look through them all one by one. Before you know it, hours have passed and nothing's been accomplished. Try not to go off on a tangent, but focus, focus, focus instead. Use whatever it is

that has distracted you as a reward for when you do get your task completed. Enjoy your newly organized space by pulling out some of those old treasures you haven't seen in a while.

Tips to avoid distraction:
- Set a timer or deadline.
- Reward yourself when you complete a task.
- Ask a friend or family member to keep you on task.

100

Organize while watching TV

If you're really having trouble with motivation to get things done, try this effective tip: Work during the commercials while watching your favorite TV program. For instance, you can clean your entire kitchen in an hour just by using the commercials to complete five-minute  tasks. Wash pots and pans during one commercial, unload the dishwasher during another, next load the dishwasher, then wipe down the counters. It's a great way to stay on track with a little TV reward in between. Also, there are many organizing projects that can be done while watching TV. You can take your filing basket into the living room to sort while watching a movie, or—my personal favorite—dump an entire drawer on the floor or table in front of you. Before you know it, time has flown by and—would you look at that—you've got yourself an organized drawer!

101

Use multitasking wisely

Now that you've read Tip 100, you're probably thinking that I'm all about doing multiple things all at once to fit more into a day. Yet, when I think of the word *multitasking,* the first image that pops into my mind is a harried mom talking on the phone, making dinner, doing crafts, folding laundry, and sweeping the floor all at the same time. While many moms are capable of this, I just can't imagine that level of busyness being sustained over a long period of time. I honestly don't think multitasking is our answer for getting more done in a day. Certainly it has its place, like when we pull out a book to read in the car while waiting to pick up our kids, or folding laundry while we watch TV. This works with simple, straightforward tasks, not those when it's important to be present in the moment. The tips mentioned in this book include many time-saving, clutter-reducing strategies, not so we can pack more to-dos into an already full day, but to allow us to slow down a little bit and enjoy some breathing space and the beauty around us.

Epilogue

As our time together draws to a close, I've got to ask: Are you addicted to the high of organization yet? My goal in writing this book was to inspire you to take the action that will help ease your burden and rid you of the stress that the clutter of modern life can bring. And what a journey it is! But remember: *This isn't a journey with a final destination; it's one that will continue as life happens around us.* With each new milestone or change we go through comes a new schedule to implement, new clutter to contend with, and new lists to detail. However, you won't need to sweat it because you've now got the tools you need to go with the flow and carry on! I would love to hear your personal story, so please feel free to connect with me through my blog, www.orgjunkie.com, and let me know where this crazy ride has taken you. HAPPY ORGANIZING!

Photo credits

All photographs are from shutterstock.com except for pages 33, 43, and 52, which are from istockphoto.com.

About the Author

© Jackie Rutsatz/Heavenly Moments Photography

LAURA WITTMANN is a professional organizer and founder of the popular blog *I'm an Organizing Junkie* (www .orgjunkie.com), a website dedicated to providing encouragement and education for organized living with a good dose of fun. She is addicted to the "high" that comes from living a life of simplicity and order and is always on the lookout for her next "fix." She lives in Alberta, Canada, with her husband and three kids.